addictive
personality

Rich Juzwiak

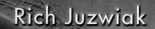

ROSEN
PUBLISHING®

New York

Published in 2009 by The Rosen Publishing Group, Inc.
29 East 21st Street, New York, NY 10010

Copyright © 2009 by The Rosen Publishing Group, Inc.

First Edition

Library of Congress Cataloging-in-Publication Data

Juzwiak, Richard.
Addictive personality / Rich Juzwiak.
    p. cm.—(Teen mental health)
Includes index.
ISBN-13: 978-1-4042-1802-4 (library binding)
1. Compulsive behavior—Juvenile literature. 2. Substance abuse—Juvenile literature. I. Title.
RC533.J89 2009
616.85'84—dc22

                                                          2008002023

Manufactured in the United States of America

contents

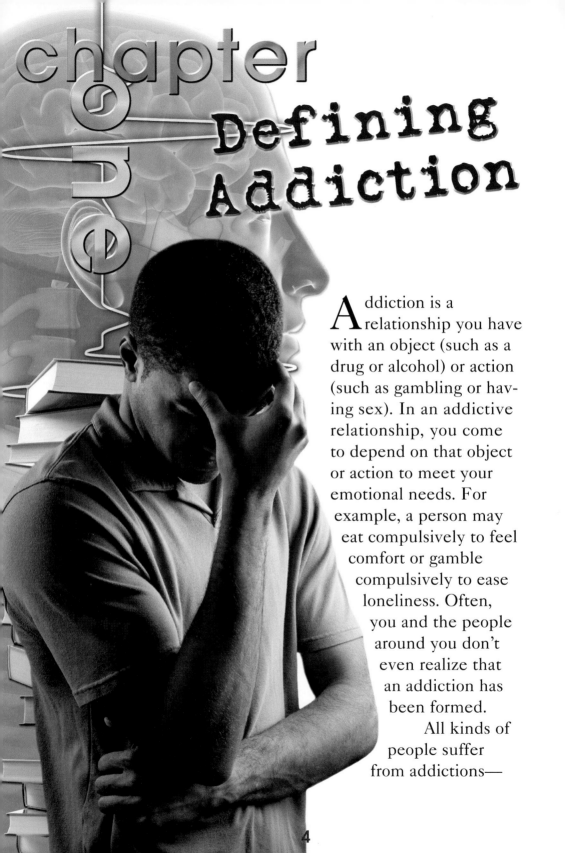

chapter one

Defining Addiction

Addiction is a relationship you have with an object (such as a drug or alcohol) or action (such as gambling or having sex). In an addictive relationship, you come to depend on that object or action to meet your emotional needs. For example, a person may eat compulsively to feel comfort or gamble compulsively to ease loneliness. Often, you and the people around you don't even realize that an addiction has been formed.

All kinds of people suffer from addictions—

young and old. There are many ideas about why people become addicted. Some theories focus on biological causes, others on emotional issues, and still others on social causes. It isn't possible to explain addiction simply. But addicts do seem to have some common traits and go through a similar process in their addictions. When these factors are looked at together, they are often given the name "addictive personality."

What Is an Addictive Personality?

There is no right way to characterize an addictive personality. Some researchers consider the concept of addictive personality controversial, as there are no personality traits that predict addiction. Other researchers argue that an addictive personality is created from the illness of addiction. It is a change resulting from the addictive process that takes place within a person. The signs of change, such as depression, irritability, and paranoia, emerge from the addictive

Some researchers believe that there are factors that contribute to the addictive process, including depression and low self-esteem.

process in the same way that other long-term illnesses can change a person's personality.

Others argue that certain personality traits make some people more likely than others to develop an addiction. For example, people who are likely to try new things and take risks may experiment with habit-forming substances or actions. Other personality factors such as low self-esteem and insecurity also play a part in addiction. If you have little self-confidence, you may succumb to peer pressure. However you define an addictive personality, a person's addiction still has a great impact on the lives of the people around him or her.

Psychological and Physiological Addictions

The more you learn about addictions and how to stop them, the better you can live a safe and healthy life. To uncover more about addiction, you need to learn about its two forms: psychological addiction and physiological addiction.

Psychological addiction is emotional dependence on the feeling a drug or action gives you. For instance, your craving for the sensations of smoking marijuana may lead you to adjust your life around getting high. When this occurs, your desire makes you feel that you can't live without it.

Physiological addiction goes beyond mental cravings. You know you are physiologically addicted to a substance when your body has a marked physical need for increasing doses. Drugs such as heroin, cocaine, nicotine, and alcohol all are physiologically addictive.

These two young men are feeling the effects of nausea and paranoia from drug withdrawal. There are two kinds of addiction: psychological (emotional dependence) and physiological (your body has a physical need for the substance or activity).

There are two signs of physiological addiction. The first is tolerance—the need to take more and more of a drug to get the same high. The second is withdrawal, which has symptoms such as sweating, tremors, and tension that appear when you stop using the drug.

Different drugs are physiologically addictive for different reasons. There is no standard time for how long you must use a drug to become physiologically addicted to it. Once any addiction is formed, it is extremely harmful.

Keep in mind that not all experts believe psychological and physiological addictions are mutually exclusive. They argue that one form of addiction brings on the other, and just because the typical signs of physical addiction, like tolerance and withdrawal, don't accompany every substance does not mean that a person is not physically addicted to that substance.

The Reasons a Person Might Become Addicted

Many factors lead people into addictive relationships. They vary for different people, and there are different theories on why people become physically and psychologically addicted.

A Genetic Link

For years, people have wondered whether there is a genetic trait passed on from parent to child that puts someone at higher risk of addiction. In 2005, scientists found the so-called addiction gene, a brain receptor that, in certain forms, makes people more susceptible to drug and alcohol addiction. Although genetic influences have been found, no specific gene has been identified, and it's impossible to predict who will and who won't develop an addiction.

While this predisposition makes it easier to predict accurately whether a person will become a drug addict or alcoholic, there is no guarantee that a person who has it will begin using. In fact, knowing that such a gene exists is most useful in providing preventive treatment that can isolate that particular receptor and perhaps decrease a person's chances of becoming an addict.

Many factors beyond genetics also contribute to whether or not someone is prone to addiction. One of the most outstanding ones has to do with family. If you grew up in a family in which at least one of your parents was addicted, you have a probability of developing an addiction.

Learned Behavior

One of the principal reasons children develop addictions is learned behavior. A large part of how you act is determined by the way your parents act. You learn by watching and interacting with them. Unfortunately, people who are raised in addictive families learn addictive beliefs and addictive logic. For instance, if you had an alcoholic parent, you learned that the way to cope with a bad day was by having several drinks to numb the pain. You grew up watching your parent drink every day, hearing all the excuses the alcoholic gives for drinking too much. You think this is normal behavior. You may grow to adulthood knowing that this is not right, but once the addictive logic has been learned, it is very hard to forget.

Emotional Escape

Internal feelings such as stress, isolation, and lack of love can send you searching for relief. Often, people turn to substances and compulsive actions as ways to escape from these difficult feelings. Many addictive relationships are ways to leave unpleasant emotions behind, but they give you a false sense of hope and security because they don't help you work through the source of your problems.

Family, Social, and Peer Pressures

Social pressures come from the external world and can spark and fuel addictive behavior. Learned behavior,

A mother comforts her daughter during a stressful time in their family life. People turn to addictive behavior as a way to escape from feelings of anxiety, tension, loneliness, insecurity, and helplessness.

socially accepted behavior, and peer pressure are all examples of social pressures.

We learn much of how to act and react through adults. When we are young, we are particularly vulnerable to their influence, and it's much harder to unlearn certain behavioral patterns than it is to learn them. If you grew up watching your father cope with his long workdays by getting drunk, then you may have learned that that is the way to deal with stress. This can lead you to rely on drinking, too, even if you know that there are more positive ways to deal with stress.

Peer pressure may also lead you into an addiction. We all want to fit in, and sometimes we end up doing things that go against our better judgment. No matter how much we don't want to admit it, we have all done things to be accepted. This is especially true when you're a teen because you are often more insecure about being left out. You may, for example, have a certain group of friends who smoke pot. They may make you feel left out if you don't smoke with them. However, if you make the decision to fit in now, your addiction may make you unable to fit in with society later.

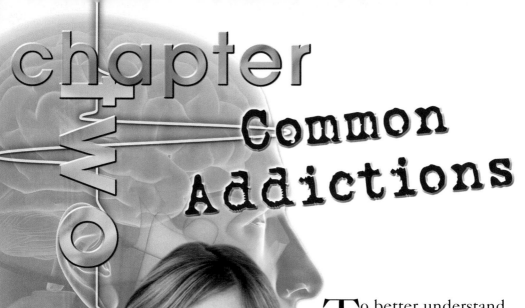

chapter Two

Common Addictions

To better understand how addiction works, it helps to know more about the most common things to which people become addicted.

Food

A common addiction that people have is to something that also gives them life. Food is a common thing to abuse because it is easily available. Overeating usually begins slowly. Often, people have grown up overeating in childhood. This pattern then becomes more intense in adulthood. Eating becomes a physical way of trying to fill an

Overeating is a common addiction. But an addiction to food can cause serious health issues if you become obese, such as heart disease, high blood pressure, type 2 diabetes, cancer, gallstones, osteoarthritis, and breathing problems.

emotional void such as loneliness. But overeating only causes a person to feel more isolated from others. He or she begins to think only about eating and often eats alone.

Overeating becomes habit forming because a person's body becomes used to taking in a certain amount of food. Therefore, it is physically and psychologically addictive, and it can be physically as well as psychologically difficult to stop overeating.

People who overeat run into many problems if they do not get help. As they become more isolated, they forget about the people and things that are important to them.

There is also a physical consequence of overeating— becoming overweight. This often creates a feeling of shame because, unfortunately, many societies value thinness as a standard of beauty. If someone becomes obese (severely overweight), overeating has physical consequences. Obesity puts a great strain on the body, especially the heart and lungs.

Gambling

Even though in most places it is unlawful for teenagers to gamble, many kids have access to gambling through Internet gambling sites, informal gambling activities such as poker games, and betting on sporting events. For most people, gambling is an enjoyable, social activity. However, what begins as recreation can have devastating effects. Many social pressures—friends, family, portrayal of big wins on television and in movies, and ads for the lottery and gambling cruises—can contribute to a gambling addiction.

Gambling has been called "the hidden illness" because it leaves no odor on the breath, no staggered steps, and no slurred speech. Yet people become preoccupied with it, spending hours thinking about past bets and planning the next one. As time goes on, the size of bets usually increases, and people find it very difficult to quit or cut back, especially if they are winning money. Losing can cause people to gamble even more because the gambler is disappointed and frustrated. The only way the gambler can become happy is by winning the next bet, so he or she keeps on gambling.

Gambling, particularly poker, is on the rise among teens, according to a 2006 Fox News report. Experts say gambling addiction may soon become an epidemic.

The effects of gambling on individuals and on their friends and family are serious. Often, gamblers lose their jobs and destroy their careers, and many end up bankrupt. Families and friends are neglected while addicts spend hours at the tables or slot machines. Gambling can also lead addicts to steal or sell drugs to pay their debts. Behavior addictions, like gambling, sex, stealing, and shopping, can lead to chemical changes in the brain, and one can actually develop a physiological addiction to certain behaviors and activities.

Sex

Sex can be a healthy part of adulthood. When sex is engaged in responsibly and as part of a relationship, it is a wonderful experience. However, if you engage in sex in an unhealthy way, it can become addictive. The addiction is a progressive process. Though researchers have not found any chemical or biological causes for sex addiction, they have found many psychological factors. Severe trauma, like sexual or physical abuse or childhood neglect, produces changes in the brain and the nervous system that can lead someone later in life to abusive behavior. Clinicians who work with sex addiction often see a pattern of underlying trauma in their clients. These include having low self-esteem, a need for escape, difficulty coping with stress, and a memory of an intense high felt during sex. Sex addicts may also become physically addicted to the feelings that are created through the release of the body's chemicals, like dopamine and endorphins, when they engage in sexual behavior.

As with other addictions, the problem escalates because of a person's powerlessness over a compulsive behavior. Sex preoccupies a person. It drives him or her to lie to friends and family, to have sex in strange places with strange people, and to continually seek out sexual encounters. Soon, the person feels out of control, experiencing a tremendous amount of pain and shame. However, this only serves to reinforce the addiction because it's the only place he or she can find relief.

Often, a person addicted to sex loses relationships, experiences difficulties at work, is arrested, has financial troubles, becomes depressed, and can ultimately lose interest in things not sexual. He or she is also at a high risk of being infected with sexually transmitted diseases (STDs) or being victimized by putting himself or herself in dangerous situations. The need for emotional release may be so overwhelming that he or she doesn't think about protection. Without seeking help, a person addicted to sex can lead a life of despair and risk catching dangerous diseases.

Drugs

One of the most visible and common addictions is drug addiction. A person who is addicted to a drug isn't necessarily dependent only on illegal substances. Also, many people who are addicted to one drug can be addicted to another at the same time.

Alcohol

Alcohol is the most widely abused drug in the world. Though technically a depressant (something that slows down the nervous system), alcohol produces a drunken high that often allows people to forget their troubles. When people are drunk, they often do or say things they would not do or say if they were sober. However, the high is short-lived. Often, when someone is coming down, he or she feels even more depressed than before drinking. This only causes the drinking to begin again.

Physical Dependency

Alcohol also affects how the body works. When a person drinks all the time, his or her body adapts itself to having alcohol in the bloodstream and then comes to need it for stability. When alcohol in the bloodstream dips below a certain level, withdrawal symptoms begin. These can be as mild as a craving for alcohol, slight tremors, and weakness. They can be as intense as vomiting, rapid heart rate, convulsions, and hallucinations. The easy way to fight these reactions is to have another drink. But that only keeps the cycle going.

Alcohol is a depressant. Drinking alcohol produces an initial high, but then when drinking is stopped, the alcoholic goes into withdrawal symptoms.

Alcohol and Genetics

Extreme cravings for alcohol can also result from genetic vulnerability. Much research has been done on the possibility of a genetic predisposition to drinking. Alcoholism tends to run in families—studies show that adult children of alcoholics are three to four times more likely to become alcoholics themselves than the general population. Generally, a person faces a 25 percent risk when he or she has one alcoholic parent and 50 percent risk when both parents are alcoholics.

While there is evidence of addiction genes, scientists point out that no one is doomed from birth—many factors beyond genetics influence whether or not someone will become an addict. Many of these factors are psychological. Not only do alcoholics become physically addicted to alcohol, they become psychologically dependent on it as well. There are several possible psychological factors. The first factor is failure in parental guidance. Unstable family environments can lead to poor decision making in children, which can cause them to experiment with potentially harmful drugs and activities. The second factor is psychological vulnerability. People who are depressed, stressed, tense, or feel an overall sense of unhappiness with their lives are often at a higher risk of becoming alcoholic because they think alcohol can ease their problems.

Environmental Influences

There are also societal factors involved in drinking. Alcohol is widely accepted in our society. Although most people know that alcohol is addictive and that alcohol abuse has devastating effects, people still drink to unwind and have fun. Only when people become extreme in their drinking habits do others become concerned. At this point, it is too late for the person to quit drinking easily.

A person may begin drinking when he or she is depressed because he or she grew up watching a parent do the same. Then, after a time, the body becomes dependent biologically on alcohol.

Consequences

A person's judgment is often impaired by alcohol abuse. Driving, riding a bike, swimming, and other activities are much more dangerous to people who are drunk. Alcohol makes a person believe he or she can do or say anything. People who are drunk are not dangerous only to themselves. If they drive, have a weapon, or become angered, they can endanger many others.

Alcoholics face numerous health risks such as damage to the heart, liver, kidneys, and brain. They also face psychological impairments such as mood swings and memory change. Also, alcoholism has devastating effects on the alcoholic's family and friends. It is almost certain that alcoholics will experience marital problems, broken social relationships, job loss, financial problems, and mental health problems, like depression and anxiety. Alcoholics come to value their relationship with drinking more than anything else.

Marijuana

Marijuana is made from the leaves of the cannabis plant and is usually smoked in the form of a cigarette or in a pipe. Marijuana is related to hashish, a stronger drug that is made from the resin of the cannabis plant into a gummy substance. Like marijuana, hashish is usually smoked.

Marijuana's effects vary greatly, depending on the quality of the drug and how much is smoked, the personality and mood of the user, and the user's past experience with the drug. In general, a state of intoxication, known as being high, results. Usually, people feel relaxed and their senses are heightened. Often, the sense of time is distorted so that things seem to take longer to accomplish. Short-term memory may also be

Marijuana is being rolled into a cigarette. The side effects of marijuana addiction include short-term memory loss, racing heart rate, bloodshot eyes, and loss of incentive.

affected. A user may walk into a room, completely forgetting the reason for being there. These effects are usually noticeable in minutes and may last up to four hours depending on how much was smoked.

Marijuana has other, more serious effects. For instance, if someone uses the drug while feeling unhappy, angry, or frightened, marijuana may heighten those emotions. It can cause an increase in heart rate, a slowing of reaction time, bloodshot eyes, dry mouth, and an increase in appetite. Marijuana also causes memory loss and a slowing of information processing. It also causes physiological changes in neurotransmitters and structures in the brain, leading to loss of motivation and cognitive impairments, among other consequences.

Marijuana causes psychological dependence. There are also sociological reasons for continuing use. Marijuana is a fairly accepted and popular drug, and people use it to fit into the crowd. This psychological addiction and sociological reinforcement can make it very hard to quit using marijuana.

Narcotics

Heroin is a narcotic, made from the opium plant. It is an intense drug that causes an initial rush, and then leads to a four- to six-hour high. During this high, the user feels relaxed and euphoric. After these high phases of heroin use, a crash comes that produces the desire for more of the drug. Other commonly used narcotics include prescription drugs such as Vicodin, OxyContin, and Percocet.

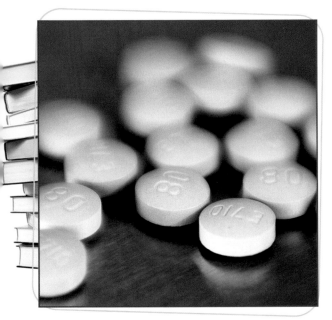

OxyContin, a prescription painkiller, is a commonly abused narcotic. Addicts develop a tolerance, meaning that higher doses are needed to achieve a high.

The use of narcotics results in both a physiological and psychological craving for the drugs. The time it takes for someone to become addicted to narcotics varies, but on average, it takes continual use over a thirty-day period. Users then begin to feel physically ill when they have not taken the drug. Heroin users especially develop a tolerance to the drug so that larger doses are needed to get high.

Withdrawal

When people who are addicted to heroin do not get a dose of the drug within eight hours after they come down, they experience withdrawal symptoms. Some people experience tearing eyes, chills, sweats, increased respiration and heart rate, and nausea. These effects can last up to three or four days. The severity of the withdrawal symptoms usually relates to the intensity of the addiction.

There are biological causes for these withdrawal symptoms. Opiates copy the functions of the body's endorphins, which help give the body pain relief. When opiate drugs are introduced to the brain, the body stops producing its own endorphins, which leads to tolerance and addiction.

Theories on Heroin Addiction

There are other reasons for heroin addiction beyond biological causes. Though many people begin taking heroin as a form of recreation, most people usually begin because they need to escape from something in their lives. They are also drawn to heroin for the somewhat romantic hopes of a life on the edge. Watching and hearing actors and rock stars in their apparently glamorous lives, many people do not see the disturbances that lie underneath. They think drug use could give them a glimpse of a better life, but this is not true. Taking heroin has the opposite effect. It more often than not leads to addiction, and heroin addiction is usually very difficult to kick and almost always leaves a trail of devastation and disappointment in its wake. Biological needs for the drug, psychological addiction, and sociological reasoning combine to make a person believe that the drug is the only important thing in life. This makes it extremely hard for someone to get help and break addiction. Using heroin leads people into a life of illegality, with the added risks of contracting hepatitis C and acquired immunodeficiency syndrome (AIDS) or death through accidental overdose.

Cocaine

Cocaine is a stimulant that comes from the coca plant. Like heroin, cocaine may be ingested by sniffing, swallowing, smoking, or injecting. Also like heroin, it causes a euphoric state, during which the user feels confident and content. Cocaine also causes headaches, dizziness, and restlessness. When it is used continually, psychotic symptoms such as hallucinations and paranoia may occur.

A cocaine addiction is dramatic. Most long-term users have marked social problems, including family unrest, employment difficulties, and legal trouble. In some cases, cocaine use can even result in death. Many of these problems result from the amount of money users spend on the drug. It often costs thousands of dollars a year to support a habit, leading people to steal and neglect their families. Women who use cocaine while pregnant put their babies at great risk for both physical and mental problems. Often, babies of cocaine abusers are born addicted to the drug themselves.

Crack, a form of cocaine, looks like chips of rock and is smoked. Laws are tough on selling and possessing it because it's very harmful and addictive.

Scientists disagree over just how physically addictive cocaine is. Some feel that because withdrawal does not cause sickness, cocaine is not addictive. The reality is that cocaine leads to severe changes in neurotransmitter action and to changes on the dopamine receptors. Other scientists point out cocaine's interaction with the brain's chemistry and the negative mental results that quitting and using cocaine causes. For example, studies have demonstrated that abusers who quit cold turkey develop depression-like symptoms. People quitting cocaine can also have memory and concentration problems, though researchers have not been able to determine exactly what causes these reactions. They do know that cocaine, especially crack cocaine, is one of the most addictive drugs available.

Commonly Abused Drugs

Some commonly abused drugs include:

- **Nicotine:** Cigarettes, chewing tobacco, and cigars. Toxins from inhaling nicotine products damage the lungs and arteries and can put the user at risk for mouth, throat, and lung cancer.
- **Depressants:** China White, special K, alcohol, narcotics, and benzodiazepines. Depressants slow down your body functions such as breathing and heart rate. They harm your ability to perceive the world around you and cause long-term damage to your liver and kidneys.
- **Hallucinogens:** Peyote, magic mushrooms, mescaline, PCP (angel dust), and ecstasy. Like lysergic acid diethylamide (LSD), a potent drug that causes changes in sensory perception, they cause a hallucinogenic trip. They can also cause permanent brain damage.
- **Amphetamines:** Amphetamine (speed), methamphetamine (ice, crystal meth, crank), Ritalin, and Adderall. These are synthetic (human-made) drugs that speed up the mind and body. They can cause permanent heart and brain damage.
- **Inhalants:** Household products containing solvents that are inhaled, producing a head rush or high. They can cause organ damage or even instant death.

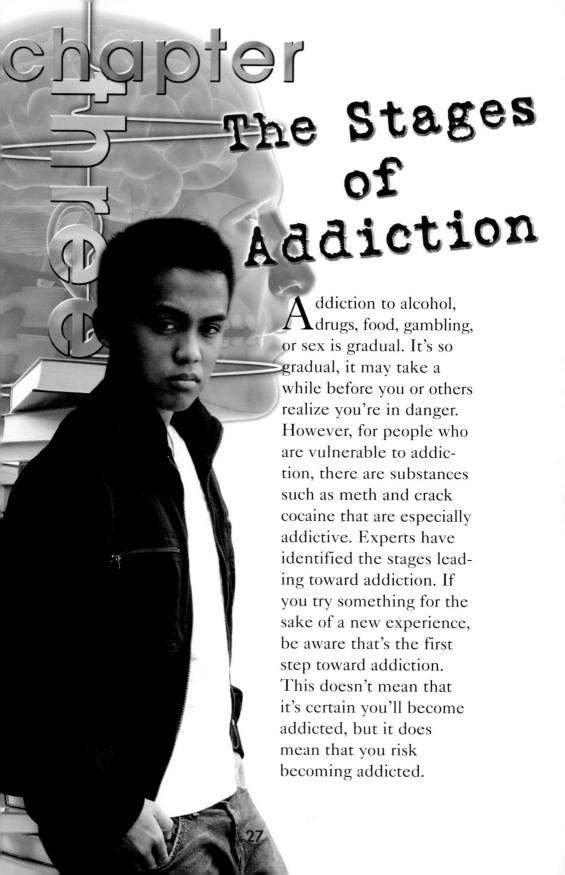

chapter three

The Stages of Addiction

Addiction to alcohol, drugs, food, gambling, or sex is gradual. It's so gradual, it may take a while before you or others realize you're in danger. However, for people who are vulnerable to addiction, there are substances such as meth and crack cocaine that are especially addictive. Experts have identified the stages leading toward addiction. If you try something for the sake of a new experience, be aware that's the first step toward addiction. This doesn't mean that it's certain you'll become addicted, but it does mean that you risk becoming addicted.

Stage 1: Experimentation

Usually, someone begins to use a drug, gamble, or have sex as an experiment. The reasons for experimenting range from wanting to escape from depression or stress to just wanting to have fun. The experimental stage is marked by doing something only a few times just to see what it's like.

Stage 2: Casual Use

Casual use is the next stage of addiction. This is marked by

doing something only occasionally. Casual use is defined as a few times a month. Someone who drinks only on holidays is an example of a casual user. Here, a relationship has been formed, but it is not a strong one yet. Most people who casually use drugs do so with small doses.

Stage 3: Abuse

In this stage of addiction, users will continue to use a substance despite the desire to quit or the negative consequences

Most begin using a drug casually and then become regular users because the urge to use is overpowering.

28

they have faced because of their use. The user can no longer control the urge to use the substance.

Stage 4: Dependence

Dependence is a more intense phase of addiction. In this stage, the person does something on a regular basis. Regardless of the level of dependence, it is not something to be taken lightly. It can easily lead to addiction.

Sometimes, symptoms associated with addiction are present in the dependence stage, including increased tolerance levels and mild withdrawal symptoms. The effects on the body, both physical and mental, and personal life can also be more intense than in the casual stage. Not only can short-term problems occur, like mild memory loss, but long-term problems emerge as well, such as financial problems for gamblers.

Stage 5: Addiction

Addiction is the final and most devastating step on the addiction ladder. It can be defined as an overwhelming compulsion for a substance or event on a continuous basis. The term "addict" is often used to describe someone who has this type of relationship with a substance or action. Addiction wrecks your life, including your health, personal relationships, and job performance. Many people who suffer from addiction have shorter life expectancies, and there is a higher suicide rate among addicts. The addiction becomes the most important thing in your life, even more important than your family. Job loss and unemployment are common.

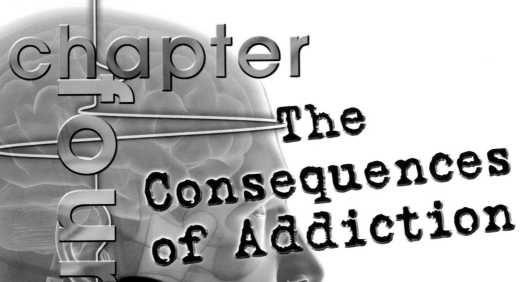

chapter four

The Consequences of Addiction

Once a person is out of control, the results of addiction can be overwhelming. At this point, addicts' lives have completely broken down. Their behavior is extreme, and their actions are even life-threatening. However, they are so dependent on their addiction that they can't control their actions.

Denial

Any problems that follow abuse or addiction are worsened by denial. The addicted person doesn't recognize that the addiction is taking over, and he

People with an addiction choose to depend more on their addiction than they do on their family members, friends, and others. They believe that their addiction brings more comfort to them than the people who care about them.

or she begins to lose control. No matter how many times he or she may be confronted about the problem, the addicted person will deny that there is a problem.

Control

Once a person becomes addicted, he or she becomes completely consumed by the addiction and often seems to be a very different person. The addict's life revolves around the addiction—he or she skips work or school and ignores normal responsibilities.

By this time, that person has given up trying to understand what is going on. He or she no longer makes excuses for his or her actions. The addiction becomes impossible for friends and family to ignore. It begins to cause a great deal of pain because trust and love are sacrificed for the addiction. Often, addicts betray themselves and others to hide from their loved ones' concern.

Addiction and Personal Relationships

An addict focuses more on the addiction than on others. The addicted person turns almost totally inward, isolating him- or herself from people who can help. The longer an addictive illness progresses, the less a person feels he or she can turn to others. The addicted person begins to feel lonely and depend more on the addiction for comfort.

Because addiction is an illness that isolates its victims, addicts begin to treat people as objects rather than individuals who have emotions and needs. People close to them may become fed up with being treated badly and may begin to keep their distance from them. In turn, the person with an addiction becomes even more isolated.

There is an emotional logic to why addiction becomes more important than people. People begin to crave the mood change caused by their addiction because it's predictable, dependable, and easily attained. People, on the other hand, may not always come through and can't always be relied upon.

chapter five

Addiction and Family

There is no clear evidence why some people develop addictions and others do not. For that reason, an addictive personality has many different aspects. Nearly all of them, however, involve a person's family.

Emotional Instability

The emotions within a family that is affected by addiction shift daily. A parent addicted to drugs, for instance, will be loving one minute and then, when he or she is high, will be hostile or abusive. Because the love you receive from your parents is very inconsistent, you may also feel unsure of the world around you. You can have a difficult time trusting other people and often expect the worst to happen. For instance, you may fear that a relationship is going to fall apart, even when there is no evidence of a problem. These feelings of doom come directly from living in a family in which things are fine one minute and terrible the next.

Physical Abuse

Addiction in families can also lead to physical abuse. People who are addicted may treat others as objects, even beating or sexually abusing members of their family. The families who experience this abuse suffer damage that can never be repaired. It leads to lifelong emotional pain.

Children in abusive families learn the habits of abuse. They grow up seeing the lack of control of their addicted parent. Even if they know this horrible behavior is not normal, they may end up imitating it, for it is the way they were taught to act. In some cases, children of abusive families end up abusing others themselves, or they keep getting in situations in which they get victimized.

Dealing with Addiction

Because living with someone who suffers from an addiction can be so traumatic, members of addictive families often look for ways to become numb to their problems at home. Children especially will do almost anything to avoid their unhappy home life. But this can be dangerous. Like the family member who has caused them so much pain, they can begin to believe that an object or action can make the pain go away. This is the beginning of the addictive cycle.

It is best for family members to talk to counselors, teachers, or relatives outside the immediate family. Only through learning about the problem and talking about the emotions can a member of an addictive family truly find relief. Otherwise, the cycle will continue.

Teens in a support group meet with a counselor to discuss their challenges with drug addiction. Talking helps people to regain control of their lives.

MYTHS AND FACTS

Myth: A person will become an addict if he or she has a parent who is an addict.

Fact: Although people who grow up with family members who have addictions face a higher risk of addiction themselves, everyone is at risk. Family life, social pressures, and emotional states are but a few of the factors that are crucial to the development of an addiction. Because no one is immune from addiction, it follows that no one is doomed either—even those with the genetic predisposition may never become addicts.

Myth: Cocaine is not physically addictive.

Fact: Not all scientists agree on the extent of cocaine's physical addictiveness, but most recognize that using cocaine alters and damages brain chemistry. Although it does not cause illness like heroin withdrawal does, cocaine does have immediate and lasting effects on the brain.

Myth: Marijuana is not addictive at all.

Fact: Anything that is pleasurable is potentially addictive. Though marijuana may not be physically addictive, it causes physiological changes, especially in the adolescent brain.

Myth: Addiction is a black-and-white issue—you are either an addict or you aren't.

Fact: Addictions don't form overnight; they operate on a continuum. Experimentation, casual use, abuse, dependence, and, finally, full addiction are the rungs of the ladder of addiction.

Myth: All addicts need to do is exert some self-control to get over their addiction.

Fact: The road to recovery is a long one that starts with a person admitting he or she has a problem. From there, many people get professional help. It may be years before a person feels comfortable enough to say he or she is cured.

chapter six

The Road to Recovery

If you have an addiction, do not despair. Recovery from addiction is possible. The goal of recovery is to break both the physiological and psychological aspects of addiction and take the first steps toward building a healthy life. Through hard work and patience, you can break away from your addiction and regain control of your life.

You don't have to face this problem alone. If you think you have a problem,

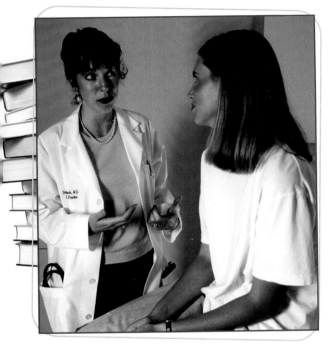

If you know you have a problem with addiction, talk to your doctor. Health professionals have been trained to assist people and can offer guidance.

talk to someone. Tell a friend. Share your concern with an adult—there are plenty of adults readily available who have dedicated their careers to helping people. Talk to a parent, a school counselor, or any other adult you trust.

Admitting a Problem Exists

The first step in recovery is admitting that there is a problem. You confront what you have been trying to ignore. Once you learn to be honest with yourself, you can learn to stop your addictive behavior and go back to living a healthy life. Slowly, you begin depending less and less on the object or action that has consumed your life.

Support Groups

Once you have admitted you have a problem, it can be helpful to join a support group, enter counseling, or find another recovery program that suits your needs.

Support groups are made up of people who share the same kind of problem that you have. Many groups have therapists or counselors who lead them. Other support groups, like twelve-step programs, are fellowships of people who share your problem. Its members help one another work through a course of recovery.

Support groups are helpful because they teach you that you are not alone. The group gives you encouragement to keep fighting your addiction. Because addiction can make

Ten Great Questions to Ask Your Counselor

1. How do I know whether I have an addiction?

2. Is my addiction physical, psychological, or both?

3. What are the short- and long-term consequences of my addiction?

4. Could my addiction kill me?

5. Could my addiction hurt others?

6. What has proven to be the most effective treatment for my addiction?

7. Should I attempt to stop my addiction cold turkey or gradually?

8. What's the nearest support group that I could join?

9. Is there a chance that my younger siblings will be influenced by my addiction?

10. What can I do to make sure I don't become addicted to more substances?

you feel separated from the rest of the world, your involvement with others can restore lost self-confidence, making you feel like a complete person.

Counseling

Counseling is another form of recovery that many people choose. You meet one-on-one or in a group with a therapist or counselor to talk about the addiction and its underlying causes. The more you talk, the better you come to know yourself. There are different kinds of therapy; some work through talking, while others work through creative expression such as art, dance, poetry, or music. When issues come up, you and the therapist work on solving them together. You can learn about what drives your addiction, how to meet your needs in healthier ways, and how to develop coping skills.

Clinics

There are other options open to you, too. Many people choose to recover at clinics. Clinics can be either inpatient (when you live there) or outpatient (when you come in during the day and go home at night). Clinics will help keep you safe while you are recovering, especially if you are experiencing drug withdrawal.

The Rewards

Recovery is a continual struggle. However, it can also be one of the most rewarding experiences of your life. You

Participating in a drug treatment program can help provide addicts with encouragement, counseling, and direction during their recovery.

learn to understand the hows and whys of your addiction and work out many of the problems you once tried to avoid. This knowledge can give you the power to confront your addictive desires if they appear again.

Through the recovery process, you can begin to feel free. This freedom can be the most wonderful feeling you have ever experienced. If you are suffering from addiction, get help. Talk to a teacher, parent, counselor, or friend for advice and guidance.

glossary

addiction Compulsive need for and use of a substance or action.

compulsive Having the effect of compelling a certain action.

depressant A drug that slows down vital bodily activities such as heart rate and pulse.

genetic Having to do with the effects of heredity.

hallucination Seeing or hearing things that do not exist.

hallucinogen A type of drug that causes the user to have hallucinations.

impairment Condition of damage to a physical or mental ability.

learned behavior Conduct developed by exposure during childhood or youth.

narcotic An addictive drug that often reduces pain and/or alters behavior.

paranoia Mental disturbance marked by notions of persecution.

physiological Pertaining to the functioning of the body.

preoccupied Mentally absorbed in a train of thought.

psychological Pertaining to the functioning of the mind.

stimulant Drug that speeds up the mind and body.

tolerance The need to take more and more of a drug in order to get the same high.

traumatic Causing stress or physical injury; a situation the body experiences as life-threatening while feeling helpless.

vulnerability Condition of being open to attack or danger.

withdrawal Symptoms such as sweating, tremors, and tension that appear when a person stops using a drug.

Alcoholics Anonymous (A.A.)
A.A. World Services, Inc.
P.O. Box 459
New York, NY 10163
(212) 870-3400
Web site: http://www.alcoholics-anonymous.org
This organization sets up support group meetings for people addicted to alcohol who want to quit. It offers free services worldwide.

Gamblers Anonymous
P.O. Box 17173
Los Angeles, CA 90017
(213) 386-8789
Web site: http://www.gamblersanonymous.org
Gamblers Anonymous is a group that helps people who want to stop gambling. Support groups can be found in more than thirty countries.

Narcotics Anonymous (NA)
World Service Office
19737 Nordohoff Place
Chatsworth, CA 91311
(818) 773-9999
Web site: http://www.na.org
This organization sprang from Alcoholics Anonymous and is devoted to helping people overcome their narcotics addiction. It is a nonprofit fellowship that can be found in more than 116 countries.

National Eating Disorders Association
603 Stewart Street, Suite 803
Seattle, WA 98101
(800) 931-2237

Web site: http://www.edap.org

This nonprofit organization works to prevent eating disorders and provides treatment referrals for those suffering from food- and body-related abuses.

National Institute on Drug Abuse (NIDA)
Public Information Department
5600 Fishers Lane, Room 1039A
Rockville, MD 20857
(800) 662-HELP (4357)
Web site: http://www.nida.nih.gov

NIDA supports research and technology to aid in the understanding of drug abuse and addiction. It also helps educate the public, health-care professionals, and policymakers via its Web site and other measures.

Overeaters Anonymous
World Service Office
6075 Zenith Street NE
Rio Rancho, NM 87124
(505) 891-4320
Web site: http://www.overeatersanonymous.org

Overeaters Anonymous is a support group for people who want to recover from a compulsive overeating problem. It is a free worldwide program.

Hotlines

Drug and Alcohol Hotline
(800) 252-6465

This hotline is open twenty-four hours a day, seven days a week, to provide information about drugs, alcohol, addiction, and treatment.

National Suicide Prevention Lifeline (NSPL)
(800) 273-TALK (8255)
This twenty-four-hour, seven-days-a-week hotline is dedicated to helping those in crisis and contemplating suicide. The NSPL is staffed with trained counselors.

Web Sites

Due to the changing nature of Internet links, Rosen Publishing has developed an online list of Web sites related to the subject of this book. This site is updated regularly. Please use this link to access the list:

http://www.rosenlinks.com/tmh/adpe

for further reading

Danowski, Debbie, and Pedro Lazaro. *Why Can't I Stop Eating?* Center City, MN: Hazelden, 2000.

Egendorf, Laura K., Bonnie Szumski, Scott Barbour, and Brenda Stalcup, eds. *Teen Alcoholism*. Farmington Hills, MI: Greenhaven Press, 2001.

Horvath, A. Thomas. *Sex, Drugs, Gambling, and Chocolate*. Atascadero, CA: Impact Publishers, 2003.

Peele, Stanton. *7 Tools to Beat Addiction*. New York, NY: Three Rivers Press, 2004.

Perkinson, Robert R. *The Gambling Addiction Patient Workbook*. Thousand Oaks, CA: Sage Publications, 2003.

Sharpe, Alan. *Drugs, Lies and Teenagers*. Camas, WA: AWYN Publications, 2001.

Shaw, Brian F., Paul Ritvo, and Jane Irvine. *Addiction and Recovery for Dummies*. Hoboken, NJ: Wiley Publishing, 2005.

Willett, Edward. *Frequently Asked Questions About Exercise Addiction* (FAQ: Teen Life). New York, NY: Rosen Publishing, 2008.

index

About the Author

Rich Juzwiak is a writer who lives in Brooklyn, New York.

Photo Credits

Cover, p. 1 (top left) © www.istockphoto.com/Liz Van Steenburgh;
cover, p. 1 (middle left and bottom left) © www.istockphoto.com; cover,
pp. 1, 3, 4, 12, 27, 30, 33, 37 (head) © www.istockphoto.com/Vasily
Yakobchuk; cover (foreground) © www.istockphoto.com/Vladimir
Piskunov; pp. 4, 12, 27, 30, 33, 37, 41 (books) © www.istockphoto.com/
Michal Koziarski; p. 4 © www.istockphoto.com/Nicholas Manu; p. 5
© www.istockphoto.com/Juan Estey; p. 7 © Jim Varney/Photo
Researchers; p. 10 © Image Bank/Getty Images; p. 12 © www.
istockphoto.com/Jason Lugo; p. 13 © David Young-Wolff/Photo Edit;
p. 15 © AFP/GettyImages; p. 18 © Lisette Le Bon/SuperStock; p. 21
© www.istockphoto.com/Leo Kowal; pp. 22, 25 DEA; p. 27 © www.
istockphoto.com/Quavondo Nguyen; p. 28 © Felicia Martinez/Photo
Edit; p. 30 © www.istockphoto.com/Tracy Whiteside; p. 31 © AP
Photos; p. 33 © www.istockphoto.com; p. 35 © Lawrence Migdale/
Photo Researchers; p. 37 © www.istockphoto.com/Bonnie Schupp;
p. 38 © Will & Deni McIntyre/Photo Researchers; p. 41 © Mark
Richards/Photo Edit.

Designer: Nelson Sá; **Editor:** Kathy Kuhtz Campbell;
Photo Researcher: Marty Levick